Return from Erebus

Return from Erebus

Julia McCarthy

Brick Books

Library and Archives Canada Cataloguing in Publication

McCarthy, Julia, 1964-
    Return from Erebus / Julia McCarthy.

Poems.
ISBN 978-1-894078-78-8

    I. Title.

PS8575.C4186R48 2010   C811'.6   C2010-903703-0

We acknowledge the Canada Council for the Arts, the Government of Canada through the Book Publishing Industry Development Program (BPIDP), and the Ontario Arts Council for their support of our publishing program.

The cover painting is by Wayne Boucher: "Ladder at the Gate", 2004, 56" X 56", oil on canvas.

The author photograph was taken by Gerard Burnel.

The book is set in Jenson Pro and Univers Condensed.

Design and layout by Alan Siu.

Printed and bound by Sunville Printco Inc.

Brick Books
431 Boler Road, Box 20081
London, Ontario N6K 4G6

www.brickbooks.ca

In memory of my parents

and the animals I've had the privilege of knowing.

And then a Plank in Reason, broke,
And I dropped down, and down—
And hit a World, at every plunge,
And Finished knowing—then—

       – Emily Dickinson

I would like to house my spirit within my body,
to nourish my virtue by mildness, and to travel
in ether by becoming a void. But I cannot do it yet...
And so, being unable to find peace within myself,
I made use of the external surrounding to calm my spirit,
and being unable to find delight within my heart, I borrowed
a landscape to please it. Therefore, strange were my travels.

       – T'u L'ung (T'u Ch'ishshui)

Contents

The White Forest

The Name That Floats on Black Water

Out of the Blue

A Mitochondrial Whisper

The White Forest

Myth never happened but always is.

– Sallust

Surrounded

There are silhouettes
moving past me   pushing light
from place to place   making room
for their shapes
since childhood I've watched them
they are sentimental
sentiment being a form of fatigue
as a painter once said

so their hands are blurred
no longer able to grasp
what they could once
they are featureless
and vague as air caught in a jar

what of the marching silence of grass
fallen on its side husked and hollow
as the small bones of a sparrow
what of the snake beneath its helmet
of rock   the tail of a mouse
a second tongue hanging from its mouth
that knows the ecstasy of fur
but cannot say

what the depths once offered us
has turned
into something else
movement
relentless shuffle of shadows
like cards with blank faces
surrounded
by the grass on its side

listening to the stillness
of the sparrow's flight
the small hollowness of bones
scratching the sky.

The White Forest

The poem lives in the white forest
with white trees   gulls in their white gloves
flying across the sky of dust

the poem doesn't know
day from night so time blurs   overlaps
like metaphor

which is the light it carries beneath its words
like a bloodstream overflowing the body
the lantern in the warren that resembles a rabbit
or a stone   oculus mundi   behind its grey curtains
the small light around its edges
like drapes catching fire

the poem sleeps in the white forest
which resembles a city   a blizzard
or large bloom of a flower that never closes
its doors

it hears a voice calling as though
it were lost
the poem isn't lost   the voice sounds
like a receding star   a chisel
dropped on the moon   or a ring placed
around Saturn   Enceladus silver
as a thurible swaying
in the shadows

around the voice the poem
makes itself   something sewn around the edges
a permeable hem made of water

a ring of dust and light to wed the space to
silence
the white forest in which it can live
like the sound of stones opening
their windows.

Flying Underground

It's where moths gather
like ashes from the moon   where small fires
of snails nudge the shadows upwards
and children play beneath the roots
singing songs   lullabies for mothers still
living above   mothers who push
emptiness like strollers down busy streets
streets lined with the singing roots of trees
and birds struck mute
by the faint lunar notes silvering
the air

everywhere we are silently tucking
nothingness in   every night
before we close our eyes   turn inward
and begin the long walk
down endless flights of stairs
stairs made of paper folded back and forth
by children   their songs pale
as moths flying underground.

On the Plain of Asphodel

Day moon   the sun's mirror
a worn coin facing both worlds at once
weathered as a headstone marking
a beginning and end that never existed

below it   cars like a burnished caterpillar
on an errand that never ends   drive in circles
metal curling into question marks
no one leaves   no one arrives   but all hurry
to deliver a message on a slip of paper
they forgot to bring

at the intersection lights turn yellow
as a hesitant sun adjusts its mirror
traffic shimmers   coming in waves
a child stands at the curb of the river
with a bundle of swimming things under one arm
and a stick like an antenna reaching for what isn't there
only then does the child step
into the intersection   walking into her shadow
the way shades walk on the Plain of Asphodel
carrying bundles and messages they no longer
remember   on a forgetful errand from the river
faces blank as coins worn down by time
from being tossed back and forth
endlessly between worlds.

Meditations on Ephemera: Dust

You're the first astronaut
traversing the ethereal moat
you catch
        on gravity's edge
Cabaletta   Cosmonaut   Caesar of air
land here
        and here
rest the aria of yourself.

Aphelion

1.
Stepchild to Pyrrha, I form stones to broken prayers,
a crude aphasia cast into orbit across a field, into the stream
and the oracular air, vigilant for the landing,
the thud through the nicked grass, the necessary splash
of finitude, emptiness's closing argument, the paradoxical proof
that distance doesn't diminish a thing.

2.
The sun is always brightest from a distance. Icarian twin, the one not
mentioned, turned his back on wax and wings and knew the closer
you got to the sun would only bring darkness. He wore the shadows
like the dark glasses of the blind. His name was Aphelion.

3.
The village of pebbles at my feet has turned off all their lights. The earth
Junes, the light clagging like a half-formed stone in a votive hand.
He comes out of the wood, the scent of burnt moss sewn
into his clothes by the hummingbird who forever seeks the dark center
of things while trying to escape its wings, and flies, a prayer into the forest of stone
leaving a single green feather behind. *Aphelion...*

4.
The tea sleeps in a pot antiqued from the ritual of itself, and dusk
gathers a slow herd of unnameable animals too gentle, too blurred, to intrude.
In the grasses and treetops, fireflies puncture the air ornate, allowing all the darkness
out, their espionage designed to answer the riddle of themselves, to find
the sequence that repeats, a chaplet of pearl, a novena of light knotted nine times
by the hummingbird's awl.
The sun is still a distance, its long body siphoning the shadows.
I form stones to broken prayers, casting them into the stream
where the sound of their entering is distinct as wings, shaking all the water off.

The Visit

I let a shadow enter
so it leaned its elbow
on my table
and cast a net
of flesh and bone far
into the room

its words were vague as vapour
its gestures slippery as though
borrowed from a realm not its own
so it watched and watched
filling itself in
a little more

its human form smiled and laughed—
a storm of crows flew from its mouth—the glint
and clem perched in the cleft
between host and host—the stunning
syllables of intent—raw Wesen of itself—

it turned my skin to scale—my blood invertebrate—

instantly annulling the meeting
so brief and black
the shadow rolled back
through the round door of its eye
like a pupil contracting
it slid down its own throat
past the outline of its heart
and there it coiled
hissed and collapsed
to its coreless core.

Angel of Loneliness

One-winged
    she limps along
unable to get completely
    off the ground
which is why you can feel the weight
of her hand on your shoulder

the soft nub
where her wing once was
throbs   a phantom ache
    coming and going
with the weather

bored
by her defiant brother and
dutiful sisters who hover in packs
like cigarettes never lit
    never burned down
she's the colour of ash
    not white like the stereotype

and she's looking   always looking
at this and that
    the rooms of want entered
and left   doors ajar   the draft
    of emptiness
blowing her sideways
    into the gust of things   bumping
her into you   into me   into the little chill
of a needlepoint ivy   green
with many envious wings.

Hibernacula

There are many places to winter when the season is too harsh
for a self to abide. I've pulled on words like an extra layer
of clothing, turned them over like stones from a cave, and entered
an aphonic place where the river exhales the sulfurous scent of
burning pyres—perfume of the dead—and branches the world.
(There's no boatman, no one to ferry me).

It's there that a membrane, fine as silence, forms along my arms
and like a daughter of Minyas I've hung in a blue frequency
aligned with rusty bells at an unheard pitch, my echolocation
a squeaky prayer woven into another layer until the temper
of weather has changed. And I fly from my father's house
in different wings, his hibernaculum in ruins like a great
turtle's shell, upside down as an empty boat, the ferryman
fled or drowned.

Twelve Red Caskets

On the anniversary of your death I leave no flowers
visit no stone   I petition no one
only the years that have escaped your life
bind my company
on the anniversary of your death I remember
no one   not even you
all I recall is how hot it was the day
you died and the dozen roses
that later arrived   twelve red caskets
to bear the memory of you away.

An Animal Sadness

It's no longer the night before
and not yet the day to come
the keys are still in the lock
the door's still open
like an arm with nothing
to embrace
the furniture sleeps beneath
its covers as I move through
the rooms of childhood

in the kitchen there's a woman
at the table counting out pills
like sorrows
she's been weeping
snaring the sadness that lives
in the dark waiting to be caught
so it knows it's not alone

the woman and the animal sadness
become one another so that her hands
tremble and twitch like paws
and its eyes are set like two blue pills
at a table in a kitchen on a moonless night
somewhere beneath the city

in the basement a man
sits in a chair with a single lamp
aimed like a searchlight at a book
at his feet there's water and a mouse
in its fur boat with four oars
the man reads
the mouse rows
the woman weeps
the sadness smiles.

In the Room of Quartz

And in the room of quartz blooms
nothingness which is a cemetery of crows
each bearing a bright yellow rose
in his beak   pallbearing the unknown
wings unfurling   petalled with dust and light
like a rose opening to reveal a room
and another and another within that.

It's not a question of space but of time
and how the walls are polished by feathers
until transparent and faceted from within
by his beak's chisel   by this smoky lapidarian.

That Mythic—Pushing

*Another way of approaching the thing is to
consider it unnamed, unnameable.*
          – Francis Ponge

Mother   Father   O abstractions
    coiled around the heart   shed humans
emptied of all that matters like skins in the grass.

Whoever you were   now gone
into who you are   and breaking
the human chain we mistake
for our beginning.

Not this father   this mother nor theirs before them.
The particular parent a heavy invention of pseudonyms
as inessential as that linguistic trick   naming—
that mythic—
          pushing into the world.

Meditations on Ephemera: Snow

Northern logos   winter's long homily
flurry of speech like an exhaled geometry
Pythagorean and webbed
as the white spider's octagonal mind
is webbed with figuring
as she clicks her glass beads
her whispers crystallizing.

Noctuary

Six O'clock

The sun's preoccupied with all the places
it's expected   it scrims the earth
the scent of burnt shadows like a cloak of crows
unfurling   hem dragging
as day departs.

Seven O'clock

The hour of reversals
things turn the darkness out
it passes its absence in the doorway:
a cat going out   a dog coming in.

Eight O'clock

Everything leans forward
silence cups its hands and walks
slowly across the room   spilling
itself here and there.

Nine O'clock

The clocks doze off
their hands tongue-tied
time becomes itself again
a small privacy   a spoon stirring
confiding its circular travels
its counter-clockwise life.

Ten O'clock

A hushed palette   colours whispering
to save their strength   a beige conversation
tinted laughter   the sound of a wave
as they fade.

Eleven O'clock

Hunched time
poker-faced   counting itself in
black as a grackle
flying into glass   calling its own bluff.

Midnight

The migratory hour   what passes
here has been before   immigrant to two worlds
night's deepest citizen.
Between its wings   the beat there is a hatchling
cusp-born   huddled and blind   its tongue a paper bag
its mouth a beggar's cup   rattle of breath and shell
rising in the sky   stars sharp as talons   hooks set
in wax   candling.
All that bright weaponry   a clutch of jacks   a glittering
heap of silver creases   the hour unwrapped
and spread open across worlds.

The Poem Is an Animal

Whose beauty is ruthless as the carnivorous night.
An animal so captivating
I secure my house with two-by-fours
and locks on every door.

I do this, not to keep anything *out*
but to keep inside what matters most—
for it's wayward and innocent as a cub
and if it wanders beyond my door
(on paws large as yellow, pads soft as myth)
it would certainly be prey for the innocence
of Man.

It would break, and never mend,
never learn to invent
anything more real than the human,
would never sigh with desire for a throat, delicate as newborn skin,
or learn to marvel at the frailty in the hunter's eye,
which is his hunger and his fear
of hunger combined.

It will marvel with teeth sharp as arrows,
with benevolent claws sheathed in silk.

Erasing the Narratives

A fresh page of snow
narrative of rabbit and coyote tracks
an old story better told
elsewhere
pine trees with the weight
of snow in their boughs
like packages from such a distance
the addresses have worn away.

I try to make something
of the wait   the hum of the undeliverable
clouding the human world
casting a shadow that can't be seen
only heard around the edges of things
like scissors sliding through tissue paper
tracing the shape of a terrible
and silent song
shaking snow from the boughs
erasing the narratives.

Meditations on Ephemera: Sun

You're the bright scurry
of a mouse across a blue field
his lantern of fur smashed in the grass.

Gestalt

Figure:

With two brushstrokes of grey
the dove paints herself into the sky

Ground:

pushing the glassine clouds into
the air's blue wings.

Poem in White

Half-bred from absence   fathered by silence
it's the colour of paradox   it rejects
the weight of the world   the burden of matter
it's the omission
of substance   it is and isn't
at exactly the same moment   it bears
its loss well having never known
anything else

white is the colour of laughter
held back   of desire waiting
the cup's regret when drained
it's the first colour   the primary wound
blindfolded   it's the bowl of ashes
you pray over   it flies
into fury   oblivious   its heat is absolute

its memory is porcelain   it dreams albino
it's the colour of a promise
before it's broken   the size and shape of
a child's coffin   a child who never existed
a funeral never performed
white is formless and void
fragile   without edges   persistent
as chaos and full of light
if you touch it you'll know absence
so profound you won't feel a thing

white turns its blind eye to the leaves
eloping with grass for winter   it's deaf
to the canticle of crows flying over
and utterly mute
to the autism of the stone
mistaking snow for its own infinite mind.

The Name That Floats on Black Water

Beneath Cyrillic Stars

The full moon is a stamp
on a dark letter
arriving and arriving
Cyrillic stars   their untranslatable script
bleeding through
as though the pen was held too tightly
pressed too firmly against the page

which is the sound time makes
rising and passing me
in its paper dress
the slight rustle
of its skirt like leaves falling off
their wooden hangers
or the sound thread makes
pulling its thin river of colour
through the eye
of a needle

all the small deaths
of no fixed address
receding in time and space
until what's left to the eye
what's left to the mind

murmurs like Heraclitean water
washing its own hair
the river's memoir
which is light left eons ago
and now arriving in small
white envelopes.

The Name That Floats on Black Water

My hands are empty
full of poverty slipping
threadbare as water
through my fingers
a solid discipline for grasping
the unseen—the nameless measuring
the named:
waterfalling

my heart is full
of space where gravity is homeless
and all the graveyards are lit
like nurseries no one visits
new light rattling through space
like flowers plunged bloom-first
through a bottomless vase
and death so ancient it can't
remember its own name
the name that floats on black water
as it's poured into the vase.

Imago

At the end
you were strapped to a bed
blankets heavy as Thomists
holding you to this earth

now your hands are still
as skin shovels thrown down   collapsed
from moving air
        from here to there
your eyes now drowned
copper as coins
at the bottom of the river

I remember how your jaw used to set
clench against what might escape your reason—
against the beating
        of your heart   fists in your blood
I remember the ripple in your throat
        a boat now gone ashore

you were the sum of an absent equation
God's scholar lost in books of straw   in the stark
centre of zero as it lay sleeping

a cloistered technician   you measured emptiness
digging into silence   dazzled by its details
and its unpronounceable names

you were all I wanted to know: father and imago
the scent of death's flowers scratch the air
an ethereal sgraffito
like the shape of your body beneath a sheet
white as a page
about to be turned.

Meditations on Ephemera: Earwig

Introvert   quiet as a doily
the colour of spilt tea or coffee
still as a Taoist
and less a braggart than the bee

Shy One   with a fierce bite
hot as the little fire
now at my heel—
O Achilles
don't you think I know
those pincers once were arrows?

Taking Leave

What would be left of our tragedies if an insect were to present us his?
– Emile Cioran

The day you died   mother
I was at the window
watching a hawk and crow lock
beaks in a death spiral
driving down like a drill
through the air
and flying apart into pieces
like halves of a single life
taking their leave of this earth

ॐ

my wings felt heavy as paper
no longer could they occupy
the air
so the trees and earth levitated
as I fell like a pebble
my antennae went blind
useless as worms on my head
all haptic knowledge lost
dissolved
like names
I never knew existed

ૐ

the day you died   mother
I was learning to read
again a poem of death
moving through its white rags and
black teeth
its salmon-scented breath
there are too many deaths
too many lives   mother
let this be your last

ૐ

sound became predatorial
all my legs collapsed
making a pyre beneath me
iridescence separated
until only a black streamer
spiralled through my mind
as my body split
like a brown suitcase full
of invisible clothes—
O terrible and final moult—
and I felt
a shadow coalesce like a great shell
like the body of my mother
darkening the sky I could
no longer see
from my deathbed here
beneath this leaf.

Phenomenology of Leaving

Description:

It begins in the mirror
drained and you   drunk on silver
seeing yourself double again
it begins with a fist
of silence   its bloodied hand
a stained calyx.

Reduction:

For one
leaving
is the slam of the door
for the other
the closing
is lush as a flower folding up
after a long red day.

This Little Black World

This little black world
is on its back
with a slender black line
of legs
like so many arrows
aimed at the twelve
as though a door
a small white door
round as a cloud of larva

this little black world
twitches and spins
like a little black planet
somewhere in a large white space
which might be the mind
at rest
or the mind in death
the little black spinning
gravity's anchor
arrowing all the worlds

between my windows
this fly
locked in transparency
is dying a little black death
all its eyes open as stars
watching me disappear
my kitchen shrink
the counter fade
the kettle   teapot   cups and mugs
disintegrate—
all the rudiments propping up
daily life—fall away

its little black lungs open like hands
close like fists   black as flowers
the frost has hit.

Something Resembling Light

You bear silence like leaves
in winter when all the earth's jewellery is under glass

your language is the sun's long breath on grass
the click of stilettos as grasshoppers
walk across the air

I know you so well
I don't know you at all
seasonless at the core   all that you are
disorients me

I'm in a forest of stars   clear-cut by rogue light
constellations scorched and curled as leaves
as small maps   O the trickery of lines
all that tangled space

meteors streak by—
my eye clots with bloodstone
and something resembling light   resembling ice
like fire in a cave which is the outline
of stars and trees that stones read by
their eyes heavy
and bloodshot from your apocrypha

ᔓ

it's easy to get lost in you
all the paths back
have been removed
pebble by pebble
stone by stone
carried off like metaphors into the unknown

their empty graves show the way
weight of what once was here
and the space it's made
shape of occupations
small earthen bowls overflowing
with the gossip of soil
the sigh of worms wedded
to the earth by their many rings
silence of ants pallbearing their dead
past my eyes beaded with maggots   eyes preoccupied
with a blizzard of mystery—
just there—where the sky clasps the earth—
the shine of a hinge only the dead can see.

Snow in August

Early August and the earth tilts
just enough for starlings
to slide across the sky
for shadows to walk sideways
across the field bruised with vetch
its blood brought to the surface

I hear the small scream
of a screen door opening

early August at the lake
I'm sitting on a rock at the point
between the coves watching
spiders walk on water
feeling myself converted

the sky is torn here and there
by gulls   by the little bit of grey
behind things
the way my mother is torn
by the grey in my father's voice

that night she is carried
from the cottage by four men
like a spider across water
her mouth full of rusted springs
opening and closing like a door
between the coves
the summer we fell out of our lives
like snow.

False Spring

With a heart resting on sparrow legs
I had loved you
with hands singed with fingertips
their ten memories of fire and water
the arson of a previous life.

With a body of blue dust I loved
the voluptuous rooms you described
the vaulted ceilings and endless view
from your house of glass.

In your perfect and impossible estate
a better season was always verging
like a false spring
luring the sparrows to nest
where they fell from the trees
softly as fingertips scorched by snow   chilled dust
as feathered rain putting another fire out.

Metallurgical Lesson

First you must anneal your material, then file, buff and blur
its edges. Your saw will unpronounce copper and bronze, its
teeth chewing on their names, considering.
You mustn't inhale the filings, that red dust, those sharp scales
unless you're prepared for a double-edged sword.

You must forge and cast your molten self, be mindful it was *this*
that named you, that gave you form, substance beyond your own.
It's undying and indiscriminate as time, that clumsy fable
that knows no end like the strand you ravel and wind
around the burnished spool, liquid as glass, crawling along the metal
road to the brittle vessel of itself.

Flux of fire, testament of breath. Breathless One, the more you
inhabit it, the less you'll be. And more.

You'll learn a difficult relief, the delicate ways of filigree.

Meditations on Ephemera: Self

Be silent   gather the stillness
that spills from all things moving
toward their death
the cricket's dark comma
in the basement
sleepers rising and pushing back
their dreams like sheets   all those silver
exoskeletons abandoned

the high dry sound of crumbling
as the wind rearranges the day

be that empty.

Blind Spot

The faith it takes to go anywhere.
I move through my days knowing
full well you're there, a little to my left
or right, steering me blind
like a back-seat driver.

But perhaps you see it differently.

My eyes fail me. It's as though you move
so perfectly in concert with me that anyone
would mistake the two of us for one.
You are there, my driver, in the place
I can't see but know is there as surely as I know
my eyes fail me. And I know you drive
through blood on circular highways that lead
nowhere, which is everywhere also.

I change directions, indicators flashing like eyes
of a fish flung onto land.
The risk of this collision is one I must take.
The scrape of metal is a bell clanging, tinny laughter
peeled from another layer,
from this timeless time coiled and spiralling through
all the layers like the single horn of a narwhal,
freeing me from this metallic corpse.

It's all deliberate
as this accident of flesh
I must embrace if I'm to get anywhere.

Return from Erebus

The field is a quiver of arrows
armies of grass   swords waving
sheathed in the green of unknown blood

I'm sitting   trying to read
but there's violence in the air   a revolution
turning before me   dividing the worlds

a reconnaissance of crows
crosses over   they land in the trees
like stabs amidst the churn and swirl
of something older than distinctions
that divide the breath   presence
more ancient than birth
or death

it hurls itself along   an ablation
of one world by another stalking form
like one divided by zero   it equals the place
where all that's parallel finally meets   these pines
black with crows polishing the armour
of their eyes   this field bright
with weaponry   the buzz and whine
of flies sawing the book from my hands   words
from my mind   words like weights   like coins placed
over the eyelids of the dead
so they won't fly
open as crows returned from Erebus
so they won't go blind as poplar leaves in sun
the shiver of their surrender in the air.

Out of the Blue

Circling like a Great Silence

(for Don)

I will never understand time; despite the fact I get
older I also stay the same. I can't understand how
things exist twelve million light years from here, *where*
is that exactly?

Some stars are dying, and in the center of their molten
death, a stellar nursery sits, liquid as life. Which means
those infant stars were already great-great-great-grandparents
by the time the picture I saw was taken, which makes my mind
go nova and this poem a sliver of light that won't exist
by the time you read it (this language will be ancient by then,
a dead tongue, primitive as lines on a cave wall
requiring at least one specialty to decipher).

Fifty million light years from here, at the far edge of Pegasus,
a spiral galaxy exhales, resembling a cloud of light like a shell
imbedded in the ocean of space. What would I hear
if I put my ear there? Perhaps the sound of horses running
and running, or birds flying and flying or maybe a poem
circling like a great silence.

That photograph I saw of storms on Jupiter looked
exactly like a Van Gogh. *How* is that possible?

Nonetheless, every morning, which are all mornings,
I push back something of the night and rise. I don't
know why, but I do, and will continue to until the night
outweighs the day. But *that's* impossible, isn't it?

Every day I rise. The First and Last Day; one endless,
infinite day with only seven names.

Tuesday

I rise on this day that is all days, infinite as Tuesday,
and perform the ordinary gestures of someone who
can't grasp time and so move with a sense of déjà vu.

I slip from sleep bombarded by light. I squint
and shuffle my way to the kettle (my great mother),
wait for it to pronounce itself (water is so articulate)
and drown the tea bags that float like pillows.
The teapot is gold as the sun (my great father),
its insides black and curved as that endless space
which contains all my mornings.

Through the window I watch cars like the shells
of large and ancient insects, drivers moving toward their day
convinced of the solidness of things, of the *before*
and the *after*. They are fighting time. Which is circling
like those dust storms on Mars, spiralling along the surface
in clouds like the grey blur of a cat chasing its own tail.

I sit before my mug of tea, egg and toast (a slice of
all the fires since the beginning of time, and all the fields of
all the grains, all the insects and all the oceans, the rain
and a little bit of dust from space), wondering if there's
anything that truly dies, if there's *anything* without meaning.

I give in, and once again crack open this egg.
It's Tuesday. World without end.

Palimpsest on a Rainy Evening

(for Valerie)

There's a lamp in a window
like a small moon framed
and hung on a house
there's rain   the sound of mice falling
and wind inventing the trees
leaves like a book
a moon on its cover
the cover opened like a window
where a small lamp is lit
and I sit writing.

Meditations on Ephemera: Poem

You're a small yellow boat
crimped to the ocean
oars lapping
sunk like tongues into the gust of things
dry birds are fluttering in the blue leaves.

You move through gilled air
pulling yourself into sight
like land not seen for a very long time
and sublime
as the sea floor finally revealed.

News from the Prosaic World

I'm always doing something perfectly
ordinary   making tea   fishing in a book
my mind hooking the flash and gleam
camouflaged by words   when the news comes

the tea grows cold as thought   the book closes
like a fin tight against itself

later I'll go outside
watch the clouds move clockwise like lids
the stars spill out their pills
there will be enough moonlight
on the water to see the fallen tree
branching the surface
like the antlers of a creature few believe in
so it only rises at night   part moonlight
part tree   part water

so it sinks again by morning beneath
the weight of disbelief   beneath the weight
of a language I never believed in
like news from the prosaic world

I'll go back inside
to the cold tea and closed book
I'll hear
the nonwords of the solitary moment
like the splash of the creature
that rose up into my life
out of nothing   out of a breath long
as a river

the creature hidden beneath the words
beneath all surfaces   who says without saying

you are mine.

Out of the Ordinary

Everyday I pray for boredom, for nothing to happen. I want a dull life
as though underwater, but even there things are sharper and the greenery,
sublime. (Once when swimming I cut myself, my blood coiled like smoke,
becoming a blurry incense for something less gentle than me.)

I pray for boredom because that blur I sometimes see out of the corner
of my eye, I know is something swimming into my life,
something trailing the shadowy ribbon of itself, but what it is
I can't say. Because I know it's lost or bored and it finds and amuses
itself with people like me. Because just yesterday the police came
to my door asking if I'd seen anything out of the ordinary
and I didn't know where to begin. So informed them
that the moon, smudged as a thumbprint, never rises in the same place
more than a few nights in a row, how sometimes it's so full
of itself it interrogates the fields and woods, cribbing light.

I identified joy's noesis, wavicles fanning out like hair underwater,
chatoyant and scunning the surface of things, a kind of molecular
showdown. And I told them how you can cut yourself on water,
of the thin shadow sharpening itself there, circling, and that it's only
a matter of time so I was glad they came. This, of course, got rid
of them. And gave me the sense that some things are never to be
as I watched the oily incense of their exhaust, a smoky ribbon
trailing my faithless prayer.

Meditations on Ephemera: Idea

Bend your Platonic knee
to the Empire of Things
the metallic breath and blood teething
bright against the shore
that gasped and shone
before your birth

Conceptual Son   O Rending One
blind your Oedipal self   assassinate your desire
to triangulate the world

fall Narcissus
from the pond's edge into
the pond

drown there   Idea
the cave's flooded
can't you feel your lungs fill
with teeth sharp as water?

This Side of the Poem

(for Mary)

Late November
      and the trees have clarified
everything
      from here the forest
resembles the pincushion
      of a seamstress preoccupied
with minimalism   with altering
      the unalterable

from here the flutter of her hands
      resembles a pair of moths   the clouds
unsewable buttons in a blue jar
      the slenderness of an aspen   a buttonhole
to pull the moment through
      and anchor it on this side
of the poem.

In the Absence of Narrative

I'm walking down a country road
a horned moon rises in the east
resembling a phone off its cradle
crickets chant their busy signals
in an evening more real than day
a day that's hung up its pastel dress
clasped its hands across its chest
and dozed off before its own blue screen

somewhere there's an open door
enough light to see the shadows by
shadows of leaves on grass like filigree
here and not here at the same time
like the shiver of a loon across a ribbon of water
or deer cloaked in dusk like the absence
of narrative

the houses are dark as the inside of teapots
sleepers curled as leaves in their beds
the dreams they won't remember are just now
assembling   taking the shapes of familiar things
impersonating the routine like a horseshoe above a door
a crescent moon above a country road
a phone off the hook
one for each sleeper calling the unknown
and walking along the hem of a road
like a ribbon of water   the shiver of asphalt
beneath slippered feet.

I Walk a Stony Path into the Orchard

Early summer and the air's soft
with rain   its wrists splashed with lilac

I can hear rain and the river
the sound of water walking on itself again

and stones underfoot like clouds grown
          heavy with thought

apple trees wear blossoms in their hair
like you once did mother   so of course you appear

          as you looked to me when I was learning to read
your eyes blue pebbles as you moved past me
in your nightgown one February blinded with snow

          running barefoot in winter's dark light
your nightgown against the snow
          white on white like a watercolour
that froze before it was painted
          your feet blue beads of ink from a leaky pen

I try not to think of you as you were then
as you are now   your mind toothless
your feet still bare
          (there are blossoms and rivers here)

I try not to think of my father's face that night
                         a sinking stone
his gaze a paperweight
               falling on my book   opened
like so many petals of a winter flower
               neither of us could name.

Thrown and Altered

(for Melanie)

Drowning in Stone

With each turning everything forms
further from itself, the closing
of a book, winter's breakup,
the hummingbird perched, a woman's
patina when her children have left home,
the stone's sweaty surface after
a night of being a stone.

Everything's just as it seems.
Nothing's as it appears.

Rivers overflow themselves, boulders
parting the flow, throwing shadows
into depths where minnows collect
and sew water to the earth.
To breathe water and air, to know the confusion
of air and the clarity of fish, the stone's struggle,
thrown and altered,
its mute cry:
just be here.
The weight of it in your ear
drowning in stone.

Offerings to the Spinner

Deer thread the trees at dusk, slipped stitches
binding presence to absence, weavers
playing colour like notes at their loom,
warp and weft, a matrix or woolly nest
where no one broods.

In the morning tufts of fur cling to branches,
offerings to the spinner, to the wheel
that never yields the same thread twice.

Thrown and Altered

Memory is porcelain, impressed
by touch, by weight, vibration shivering
the surface, here and there folded
as an envelope, containing the
uncontainable.

It has neither tooth nor bone
and collapses in a breath.
You can never deceive it.

It remembers the weight of stone,
the crushing touch that made them cousins.
The stone's tossed, porcelain thrown.
One is absentmindedly itself, the other becomes,
never forgetting all its forms, fluid
as glass, translucent as history's turning leaves
tossed and spun into whatever comes, fading
into air, pale as deer in their trickery
binding the trees
with dusk.

Behind the Poem

It's poemless after all—like the scarred chest
of a breastless woman kissed, the smile
on her lips a crescent. It's the cuttle of two stones
huddled in the snow, the flint of their secrets.
Or leaves in autumn, scores of colour in the air
and the soft songs of their falling.

It's the sun-begged snow sharing the burden, its blue light
crevassing itself, the small moan as it goes. It's the poetry
behind the poem, so many times removed, so many times
diluted with words so that this is nothing at all like what
it means to say, nothing at all like what started it
in the first place: the *waw* of a breath all around, rising
and falling like a chest scarred with kisses.

Rain in a Small Room

(for Anne and Fred)

It's the pull to the body's window
the reach
for what hovers just beyond
the flesh
water's crease as it catches
light   this page folded into a room
of windows through which hands pass
pale as cups   as a splash
of birds against the glass.

The Larger Field

(for Miki)

The sun slips like a knot
shadows bleed across the field
like wounds masking pain

I live in a grass house and knit
as insects do in the larger field
I darn the air the colour of dust
so it can know itself
and embroider the borders so I know
which world I'm in

I knit what no one wears
like emptiness arranged in a clear glass vase

between the blades and stitches
light with her needles   with her glint
and mask of blue wool   stabs my house.

Out of the Blue

(for Gwendolyn MacEwen)

It's the fastest colour—
driven out of nowhere   no body of its own
to rein it in
it's large and ancient   the colour both touched
and sound—overflowing everything into which
it just can't fit   it's a gush—
rushing from the root of thing to thing
it's not the colour of coming or going
these are plain and slow as yellow
it's the clonic colour of the whelm
bearing more dimension than air   its hair
is static   a shocking blur   it's the highest temperature
reached in a blink—exhausting—the tinted atmosphere

it transfixes with its cobalt stare   slapping into you
again and again   an ocean to a stone   a currency submerged
it's the bully sharpening itself   a bolt
of metal reaming its tinny charge   its molten mutiny
cooling into a stick still lit with the scent of fear

it's the colour that can't find its way home
the lost one   its way forgotten
it's a streak   the colour with no clothes
a failed invisibility collapsing into being—
a bruised prostration   a simple vigilance

I want to take it in my lap   stroke the static from its hair
and ground it in a body of croons
I want to pat its fiery hands down and bandage up
its burnt feet   and tell it   *no matter what   no matter when
my door is always open.*

A Mitochondrial Whisper

Things keep their secrets.
— Heraclitus

Kundalini Rising

I remember my bodies the way this desk remembers the oaken log
and tree, the sibling forest from which it came. I remember
the basements in which I've dwelled, moleishly nudging
the shadows through tunnels, lumbering from den to den,
a worker ant with the weight of a crumb like a house balanced
on my back.

I have lived above, becoming a hundred eyes of a glass house,
nothing escaped my notice, the sun opened and closed
its third eye on the world. The cabochon moon set its amber
until my insect self became transfixed and lapidescent,
encased in its protective glow.

I've lived without windows, in a house black as onyx, becoming
all ears for tarantula sounds, sprouting antennae to feel my way
around, and marvelled at how muted and soft the world becomes
when the body is robbed of glass.

Now the house I inhabit has many levels. From the upper rooms
the moon is a thousand suns and I live vertically for the first time.
Uncoiling, I ascend from den to attic nest, kundalini rising.
Meeting all my former selves, I slide past branches on the tree
giving roost to the delicate birds of memory, my tongue putting out
the fire in my mouth. I ascend my former bodies, pale as skins along the bone
stairs, and brush the sand and flies, the birds and flying ants
from my mind with a hand finally free to shade my eyes.

Poem in Grey

It's neither here nor there
it contains white's mania   dilutes the arrogance
of black   robbing it of martyrdom   a thief of definition
the colour of the falling
it reins in the speed of blue and ignores red's hysteria
(which only makes red see itself more—furious narcissist
passion's cliché)

it's infinitely moody but patient with its many shades
it shies away from absolutes   blurs the lines and rubs
all the edges away   it doesn't have a leg to stand on
loses all the arguments   and smoulders

it's the colour of dusk and first dawn
it's neither now nor then
it's the between place and between time
the *where* and the *when* the other colours fear
unable to empty themselves   clinging to definite space and line
it's the quietest one   muted by seasons
sharpened on stone   seasons so bright and polished
it must shield its tarnished eye

it tastes like a cup of smoke after a long walk
on embered ground   the sighs of singed flesh
a difficult incense rising   twisting into doves who fly
into nothing
it's the sound they make as they go
the purr from the invisible throat   a throat lined with feathers
the colour of sleeping heartbeats   of a wave splashing
a rock's face trying to wake it   disturb its solidity
the more it tries   the harder the rock sleeps   flying in grey

it's the feel of a string slipping from a finger   the moment's haze
rubbing up against a leg   the body's fugue   the dusty rib
dimly recalled as circling doves
as smoke rings

in an unwashed cup.

The White Moose

Is born of water and ice. Niveous, he swims up
from the place we all know,
the lake covered by a sheet
like furniture in the off-season.
A hatchling from the frozen lake, he's the reverse
of a drowning.

He comes running, sleek with birth,
white-hot, the shock of steam inventing
the winter air, his nostrils flared.

The white moose, shaking off his confusion like a caul
walks toward the shore,
melting into the snow banks.
I follow him, northing
toward moose and snow, magnetic palimpsest.
My movement, an avalanche in reverse,
the sound of snow breathing, the hoof in the vein
    descending
        and descending
niagara of white—this exquisite trampling.

A Mitochondrial Whisper

(for Elaine Campbell)

The poem lives in a forest
black and thin as the circumference
of zero turned sideways

the poem isn't a poem here
it isn't made of words or the silences
they're written on
it's complete and alone
unpoemed
subtle as dust on a grey feather
as the small burn it feels
like a mitochondrial whisper along a nerve
it doesn't have

the poem is patient
in the thin black forest which wraps
around the white one
like a crow's wings in the downbeat
turning the inside out
containing the infinite

it knows it will grow a body of its own
sounds   words will form
and reform   silence will slide beneath
it like water   like an unfathomable bird
liquid with flight
it knows it will grow
down into the world
carry its language into this one
like coins   flowers or scarves the colour of doves
turned out from pockets and sleeves
no one sees   apports
falling from the zero
white as rain   black as the pure north

of the Aztecs
landing as words
as hand-me-down clothes
on what has taken lifetimes
to disrobe.

Diabolos

I don't know if what we name evil is a streak
in nature gone berserk
Thanatos swimming back upstream
an infinite desire
an uncontained hunger in the vein—
the daimon we divided come home
holes for pockets
rags in its heart and ten drops of blood
where its claws were once.

Is it renegade cell or fugitive force
tapping its blind cane in the shadow's heart
like the thrum of an immensity
desiring form
the roar of blood and air
the snort of those famous horses
I grip against—
their eyes large and bright as fires out of control—
as diabolical as the poem
before it's written.

I Do Not Know Your Name

I do not know your name
but you're there like the moon
counting stars like change.

How long have you been there?
Since fire was invented?
Since mammals began to dream?

I do not know your name
but you've been with me
since the beginning—before

I fell into my body's shadow,
its blood dug into the earth's
tissue, the rooty sinew like a string

tying both skies to my mind.
I've dreamed of you for decades,
felt you there beside me,

a whisper beneath my skin,
scented you in the underbrush,
heard you moving like fur

against leaves
in a frequency that pains me.
You follow me like

a name.
You're the synaptic kick and exult
of form before form, liquid

as the ripple beneath
the face across from me
when it laughs.

You're the husk and ash—the collapse—
and the fire
of the comet trailing there—

the flash
of death passing—
which is time with all its secrets kept.

Psalm

There's a man surrounded by crickets in the grass
he's sitting on damp soil   its breath better known
than his own heartbeat   he's sitting with a congregation
of stones   listening to the earth's sermons   all the readings
from the scriptures of grass which were written in secret
composed of stalks and blades and glyphs of light
and the legs of crickets like bows against strings
playing the psalm of themselves
the man sits   oblivious to the beauty of his own solitude
which is a single blade of grass in the evening breeze   genuflecting.

Legerdemain

I'm sitting in the woods
on the knuckle of a pine root
where I can eavesdrop on the river
talking to itself
wildflowers are closing their blue eyes
the sparrows rearranging the dusk
dayshift giving way
to night's
shadows driving up
in their big black cars

the pines sharpen like stars
with all their lives contained
one inside the other
with all their memories of dust and rain
of the unimaginable space
between darkness and light
which is like the space in a frog's body
crouching between water and land
between land and air

beetles black as shrapnel
bookmark the earth where I sit
roots of pines reaching through the deaf soil
bright as hands signing light
legerdemain of all that passes
and all that appears

these pines open as doors
    that space which is
the brown static of pheasants
changing frequencies and
the battlefields of silk between boughs

where the light of a moth is turned off
by a spider

an owl sits in her cave
of feathers
her eyes opening like handcuffs
as she contemplates
pulling a rabbit out of its earthen sleeve
and plucking mice from their shadows
shadows that still run along the edges of the abattoir
listening for the swing of the blades above
the world's dark puppetry.

Meditations on Ephemera: Fly

Doped on summer   stung
by the chill coming on
put away the little black book
of yourself   no one's returning
your calls

Inkling   Flying Chandelier
Iota of Death dressed in leather
pallbearing the maggot's dream
Little Twitch   Punk of Air
scribble your body's note
your asterisk self
toss your cap and gown
graduate!

The Clouds Reach Down

Clouds scar the sky   sparrows scatter
like ashes above a green fire

the clouds reach down   take root   bind towns
and cities to a dream of towns and cities

they reach under the ocean   sinking
like stones   bouldering to the sky below
the sweep of their breath like the afterthought of a comet
or the swirl inside the mind of a snail
a swirl green as the dress memory wears
as it's born in the forest

a forest immense as the waking
on a foreign shore   the thrash and slap of land
the choke and coil of carbon naming itself
its history of fire   the molten kiss and rain-soothed char

each tree sleeps   tentacled as an octopus
a heap of liquid sticks smouldering
into clouds   into ashes that drift
like sparrows onto this page.

What We Reach For

It's the way it laps against my house, spilling
through cracks and seeping under doors.
I reach for the poem always, a vessel to float
and bob across the river no matter what the weather.
It's both vessel and river and the way they travel together,
where the line of one curves into the other.

The watermarks on my skin
don't alarm me. Each time I drift a little further,
soon my eyes will be wavy as hair, my words
submerged in the element they trace, a mere signature.
I'll read by the light of a fin and reach into
the silence which is smoke drifting in light...
I can't see it but know it's there, the faint scent
of something burning in the bright air, a whisper
like the slow leak of a world where
everything is brilliant and pained.

It moves through me like water
and the colour of my life is changed.

The Drown

"...so in this
immensity my thinking drowns,
and sinking is sweet to me in this sea."
            – Giacomo Leopardi (translated by W.S. Merwin)

Rain types all day

to the west the sky sulks in its heavy grey dress
to the east clouds pale as buttons fastened on blue

blossoms mumble: *pink   white*
elsewhere I've tried and failed to speak *white*
the absent slang of snow's dialect
I've tried and failed to whisper *grey*
felt the sleight of its watery vowel in my mouth
like a mirage—
blue unwraps its bolt
of fabric   an electric
river I swim never touching bottom
or the phosphorescent streak of its one verb
already light years from here—

but I know nothing of pink
its petals erasing the rain
its leaves broad and sharp
as propellers
the churn and urge of green
        the slow bleed of land
into my sight   the drown of yellow just there.

The Weight of Who You Are

You come to me as you always do,
your arms weighed down
with the emptiness of myth,
all the small nothings we believe,
the strands we twist and braid
into a make-believe weight
like the weight of paper
blowing away, little scribbles in the air.

Mother, the black braid you wore
coiled as a crown of sleeping snakes,
rattles like jewels, the glint of hairpins
like fangs sunk into the rope of itself
in an infinite feast,
has finally left its skin, an offering
in the bowing grasses
robed in wind.
You no longer touch anything
more solid than air, the world like a chair
fallen away

your braid become strands again,
the rattle of jewels in your blood's crib
lulled, the diamond bite, the garnet sting
no longer braided into endurance, into belief,
into the shape of your arms, empty
and slender as bracelets
on wrists of air.

When the White Dove Appears

The leaves are waking in their hammocks
the sun's yellow boat floats upwards
I'm sitting on my deck
drinking tea from a chipped cup
jays smash like blue china
flung into the trees
and fly away mending themselves.

It's a morning like any other
a book in my lap
and the fury of the real
written before my eyes.

At my feet
a mandala of sand
like a small ball breathing
newly hatched spiders
expanding and contracting
both wave and shore
in a universe made of silk.

When the white dove appears
there's an omen of grey in her feather-tips
like early typography
her body is a brush
painting a space amidst the rust and ochre
coloured roof   a stroke of white
like a chip in a brown cup
the cup I drink from
on a day like any other.

November's Conversion

The days begin to recede like a breath
half-breathed.
This is the month that invents all the shades of grey,
that smudges the sky and rubs the edges of clouds away.

But my eyes grow bright as though they've stored
some previous light I no longer remember and only now
arrives—

it wells up, a mysterious conversion
(my ivies breathe heavy greens—
a last dash for furious growth before the sun becomes
a memory in the distillery of their leaves),

and my deepest eye exchanges colours, surrendering
its galaxy of black to seasons of blue and grey and white
(in winter's implosion I'll search for the edges
of my world with many green hands).

Poem in Black

It's the flag of arrogance flown at half-mast
it's the Cartesian colour whose first word is *I*
the Newtonian despair of cog and wheel   an existential creed

it's self-centred and worships absolutes   pure definitions
it's so young it doesn't remember how to surrender
and sings   *this is the fire from which I came*
its heart made of kindling   its wings brittle
burnt   disintegrating
it's the colour of the lie (not white which is the lie
of the lie) the charred smile as it's told
it's the colour of contempt
for all things outside its sphere of influence

it's the colour that wouldn't   the fallen one
always charismatic   it persuades all the other colours
to come home   that it can't live without them
it's the scent of tricksters and priests   self-proclaimed intermediaries
marking the god-tree
it's fast as the dart of the serpent's tongue hitting two marks at once

it's the size of the drawer you store
the horror in   the shape of the key locked within
the sound of the tumblers like coffin lids closing
tired canthi of eyes that have seen too much

it's the shape of one person
having to bend into the longest night

it's the shadow white casts   the shade of yin's past   muscling into the moment
like a wave   rising and falling   rattling shells and stones so it can know itself
it's the shape of a claw drawing blood   a small feast   the clatter of bones like cutlery

it's the bruise's memory   turning out the light
it's the idea of the cave   the sound of that rending
an echo   the sex of two sticks   primitive   those first sparks
the knuckles of death's clenched hands.

Meditations on Ephemera: Metaphor

Wolf in the palace
of grass
priest without religion
ruler of kingdoms not yet
invented
you're the guerilla in the hills
resisting

you splatter the trees
with dusk   their outlines fading like old kings

     I pray the wolf my soul to keep

the grass retracts its green claws.

A Brightly Coloured Ball

(for Marlowe, Pooka, and Wodwo)

The moon is on its shelf
my cat is curled like a shaving of a cat
he's closed the curtain of himself
to travel in privacy
his heart made
from the shadows of birds
his tail ringed as a tree
in the primeval night
his mouth of nails
where photographs of teeth
hang like lunar stalactites
and his mind
stuffed with bright
bits of yarn rolled into a ball
a brightly coloured ball
that rolls and rolls
like a planet turning
in and out of light.

Ontological Slang

And that my words are the garment of what I shall never be
Like the tucked sleeve of a one-armed boy
                        – W.S. Merwin

I come here
for the relief of the page
for the void
holding me up like a single blade of grass
for the hollow in the hills the colour
of smoke in a cloudy vase

I come to open the letters
in a mother tongue I've forgotten
the lisp of a moon in the morning sky
above the wet huddle of stones
grey as bundles of washing

I'm here because the violets turn toward the window
so many purple suns in a room small enough
to contain the passing of light and time

pulling the sun down like a blind on the landscape
where shadows hurry home
ahead of the dark and bats spill out
of their sleep like dusk

I come for the sound
of violets turning in early March
when the earth is in its hand-me-downs
and snow turns back its cuffs

I listen to the overlap   the husk of one world
food for the next   in the clearing
that precedes language
where words are ghosts of being   empty as clothes
pinned to the line above

the ripple of siskins muddy as water
the ooze of a slug's wound
and the storm seeping
from the violet's mind
in a forest where a river drowns nightly
its pockets full of stones   its mouth full of boulders
ontological slang like the rush of shadows
across a page   the phantom speech of a heron flying over
grey and frayed as a sleeve.

Notes

"On the Plain of Asphodel"
the plain of Asphodel: The place in the underworld where most of the shades dwelled.

"The White Forest"
oculus mundi: Literally, 'eye of the world'; also refers to a circular window in sacred architecture.
Enceladus is one of Saturn's moons.

"Aphelion"
Pyrrha and Deucalion survived the great flood and were counselled by the Oracle near Cephisus' stream to cast behind them their mother's bones. The stones he threw behind him became men; the stones she threw, women.
clagging: To clot or clog, derived from 'clay'.

"The Visit"
Wesen: German noun, usually translated as 'essence' though Heidegger used it to mean the way in which something pursues its way, how it remains what it is over time.

"Hibernaculum"
The daughters of Minyas were weavers who were punished by being transformed into bats.

"Noctuary"
candling: A method in embryology where light is used to see through the shell of an egg; also a ceramic term, referring to a firing where low, constant heat is applied for a long period of time.

"Return from Erebus"
Erebus: Literally, 'deep blackness/darkness or shadow'; Erebus was in some Greek myths the outer realm of the Underworld through which the dead passed before entering Hades.

"Imago"
sgraffito: Literally meaning 'scratched'; a technique in painting and pottery where a surface layer of paint or glaze is scratched through to reveal another contrasting layer beneath.

"Meditations on Ephemera: Poem"
Italicized line is from Wallace Stevens' "The Pure Good of Theory".

"Out of the Ordinary"
noesis: The act of perceiving as opposed to *noema*, the object of perception.
scunning: Originally a nautical term meaning to move rapidly across a surface.

"Diabolos"
diabolos: Literally, 'to tear apart' (*dia-bollein*); the opposite of *symbolic*, a joining together, both aspects of the daimonic.

"Legerdemain"
legerdemain: From magician's vocabulary, medieval origins, meaning sleight of hand.

"A Mitochondrial Whisper"
black north of the Aztecs: In Aztec culture colours alluded to a space, a time, particular gods, some stars, and a destiny; one was born under the sign of a colour; black was associated with darkness, cold, drought, war, and death; its space was north.

Acknowledgements

I would like to thank the editors of the magazines in which some of these poems first appeared: *The Antigonish Review, Arc, Contemporary Verse 2, The Fiddlehead, The Literary Review of Canada, Atlanta Review* (USA), *Dream Catcher* (UK).

Grateful acknowledgement to the Nova Scotia Ministry of Tourism and Culture for financial assistance.

NOVA SCOTIA
Tourism, Culture and Heritage

I'm most grateful to Wayne Boucher for his kind and generous permission to use his painting for the cover.

Thanks to everyone at Brick, especially Barry Dempster and Alayna Munce.

Once again much thanks to Don and Mary.

Julia McCarthy is originally from Toronto. She spent ten years living in the United States, most notably in Alaska and Georgia. She has also lived in Norway and spent significant time in South Africa. She has one previous collection of poetry, *Stormthrower* (Wolsak & Wynn, 2002). She now resides in Nova Scotia where she works as a freelance writer and editor.